Hello, I'm an archaeologist.

I study the way people used to live in the past by examining the things they have left behind – the homes they built, the objects they used and even the skeletons in their graves. If the period I'm exploring is far back in time, these things will have become buried under many layers of soil, building rubble and all the other stuff that people chuck on the ground and leave. Over the centuries, this builds up to quite a thick layer. That's why, when we think of an archaeologist, we usually imagine someone exploring the bottom of a hole that they have dug in the ground.

Historians dig into the past in a different way. They study writings from the past to discover what happened when, who did what and what they were thinking when they did it. However, sometimes there are no written records for them to study, and this is the problem they have with the first two centuries of Anglo-Saxon history. Before 597 (when the Pope sent his missionary, Augustine, from Italy to convert the Anglo-Saxons to Christianity), they had no alphabet that could record their spoken language. They had written symbols, called runes, but these were used for magic charms or for inscriptions by craftspeople; you wouldn't use them for recording everyday events.

Luckily, we archaeologists can help fill the gap. We have discovered many interesting Anglo-Saxon remains from this time period. At West Stow in Suffolk, the ruins of an early Anglo-Saxon village have been found and rebuilt, and it is now a museum you can visit. In the British Museum, you can see the treasures that were discovered in a pagan ship-burial found at Sutton Hoo in Suffolk. At Yeavering in Northumberland, archaeologists have found a large site with many buildings, including an impressive royal hall!

We can find other clues about the early Anglo-Saxons by looking at the objects they buried with people when they died. Knowledge of other similar peoples, such as the Vikings, can help us to make guesses about the Anglo-Saxon way of life. We can also read what later Anglo-Saxon writers had to say. Unfortunately, most of these writers were monks who weren't really interested in everyday things. However, historians have been able to learn a lot about the Anglo-Saxons from books written by their most famous author, the Venerable Bede. In one of his books, Bede tells the legendary story of Hengist and Horsa, thought to be the first Anglo-Saxon conquerors. You can find out more about Hengist and Horsa at the end of this book.

First published in the UK in 2011 by The Salariya Book Company Ltd
Originally created and designed by David Salariya

Revised edition published in the UK in 2025 by Hatch Press,
an imprint of Bonnier Books UK
4th Floor, Victoria House
Bloomsbury Square, London WC1B 4DA
Owned by Bonnier Books
Sveavägen 56, Stockholm, Sweden
www.bonnierbooks.co.uk

Copyright © 2025 by Hatch Press

1 3 5 7 9 10 8 6 4 2

All rights reserved

ISBN 978-1-83587-146-1

Edited by Rebecca Kealy
Production by Nick Read

Printed in the UK

You Wouldn't Want to...

Be an Anglo-Saxon Peasant

Written by Jacqueline Morley
Illustrated by David Antram

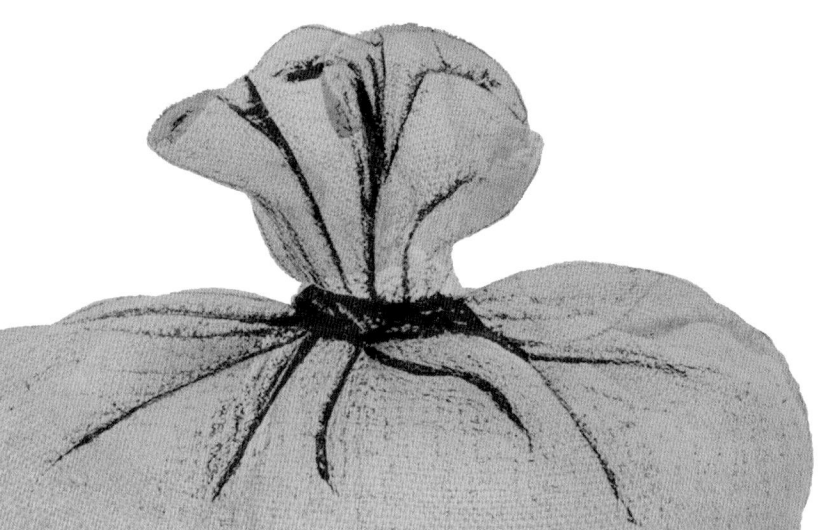

Contents

Introduction 5
Village life 6
Home sweet home 8
Keeping everyone fed 10
Paying tribute to the king 12
Going to market 14
The old gods 16
The coming of Christianity 18
Blood feud 20
The folkmoot 22
A bad year 24
Fighting to the death 26
Celebrating victory 28
Glossary 30
Index 32

Introduction

You're a farmer's son living in England in the early seventh century. Your people are descended from the Angles, who were invaders from northern Europe. The Saxons and the Jutes, who arrived about 200 years ago, also seized land from the native Britons, and made themselves at home here.

Before these 'Anglo-Saxons' took over, Britain was part of the Roman Empire and British people copied Roman ways. But when the Roman legions were called home to defend Rome, they took their knowledge and skills with them. By the time the northern invaders arrived, Roman towns, roads and farming estates had all crumbled away.

The Anglo-Saxon invaders were farmers and warriors whose leaders fought each other for land and power.

They are still fighting each other in your day, and you live in fear of raids at night. Your home is a poky wooden hut, and you spend every day slaving away in the fields just to have enough to eat. You really wouldn't want to be an Anglo-Saxon peasant!

By 600 CE there were five main kingdoms: Northumbria, Mercia, East Anglia, Kent and Wessex. Your ruler is King Edwin of Northumbria.

Village life

This is your village. There are about 20 wooden houses clustered around a much larger building, which is the great hall of the village overlord. The lord is a powerful warrior who leads a war band of loyal fighting men. These are high-ranking people, known as thanes. Ordinary villagers like you are ranked as ceorls (pronounced 'churls'). Apart from having to make certain payments to your lord, you are free to live as you wish – unlike some villagers who are treated as slaves.

Although ceorls are free, they haven't got many choices in life. They have to build their own houses with timber from the woods, and they have to grow crops and raise animals if they want to eat. You have no spare time to yourself as you spend all day helping your father with his cows and sheep, or working on his strips of land in the nearby fields.

The water you use is all carried up from the river. This has been your job ever since you were big enough to carry the buckets.

House frames are made of strong posts set into the ground, strengthened with timber beams. The walls are formed of wooden planks, or 'wattle and daub'. The roofs are thatched with straw.

Wattle and daub is made by weaving together small wooden branches, which are then plastered over with a mixture of mud, straw and pig dung. Plastering is not your favourite job!

Pooh!

Handy hint

If your house is draughty, stuff the gaps between the planks with wads of sheep's wool.

Your thatched roof is starting to show signs of age. A new layer of thatch on top will help. You carry up bundles of straw which your father fixes in place with 'staples' of bent sticks.

Most families have a vegetable patch near the house for growing leeks and beans, and a fenced-off area for pigs and poultry. When the pigs push down the fence, you're the one who has to mend it.

Home sweet home

It's dark and smoky inside your house, even though the door is usually left open to let in some light. The draught from the door sends smoke from the open fire into your eyes and down your throat. Even so, your house is one of the best in the village because it has two rooms. There is a partition dividing the living quarters from a room at the back, which is where your parents sleep. In the main room, your mother, your sister and the slaves are always busy. There's food to be cooked, corn to be ground into flour and clothes to be made. Your mother and sister take turns weaving cloth on the loom by the wall.

Smoke is supposed to escape through a hole in the roof but in reality it gets everywhere! You're used to the flavour of smoky stew.

The stew pot is on the go non-stop with new additions from day to day. Usually, it's pottage – a mixture of boiled cereals, leeks, onions, peas and beans.

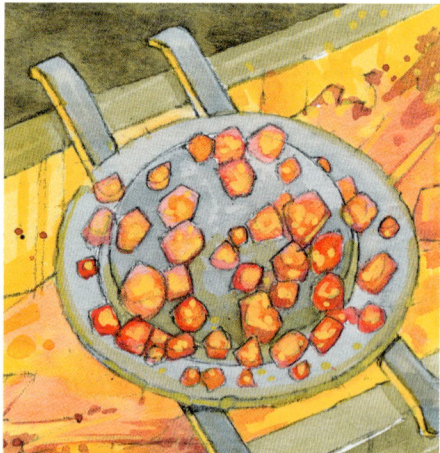

Loaves of bread are baked on the open fire under an up-turned pot, with hot embers heaped all around it and on top.

Handy hint

If you need the loo, there's a hole in the ground round the back!

Ouch!

Because of the embers, the bread is often full of grit. This gradually wears away the enamel of your teeth and gives you toothache.

When your sister's not weaving, she's either spinning, milking, making the butter and cheese or preserving food for the winter.

There are two slaves to help. Slaves are mostly people captured in battle. They can save up to buy their freedom or a kind owner may decide to free them.

Keeping everyone fed

Cold hands, raw face, numb feet – it's no fun stumbling along behind the plough. Your father is never tired of telling you how lucky you are. His father had to use an old-fashioned scratch plough which was useless on heavy soil. Nowadays, farmers have a new type of plough which cuts deep furrows and turns the soil over at the same time. It's very heavy and needs four oxen to pull it. No one can afford to own that many, so people share their animals and take it in turns to plough.

At dawn, you open the sheep fold and drive the flock out to graze. They have to be carefully guarded all day in case of an attack by wolves.

Can we have a break soon?

Everything around you is put to use. The nearby woods provide timber for building and your pigs can forage for food among the trees.

Cow pats are welcome, even when you step in one! They provide a rich manure, so cows are put to graze where next year's crops will grow.

Handy hint
Don't waste your own waste. It makes a great fertiliser!

Hunting provides a change of diet and a welcome outing for you. With a bow and arrow, you can bring down hares, wild geese and even deer if you're lucky.

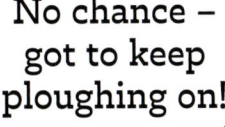

"No chance – got to keep ploughing on!"

The fields must be sown by hand. You take the seed from a pouch hung over your shoulder and scatter it from left to right as you trudge across the fields.

The bees are your responsibility. You hate being stung but it's worth it. Without honey, nothing would taste sweet and there would be no festive mead to drink.

Paying tribute to the king

Your king is here with his war band. Throughout the year, he travels around the villages in his kingdom, forcing villagers to hand over their stored food supplies and staying for as long as it takes to eat and drink the lot. The food or money collected is known as a 'tribute', or tax. Thanks to these tributes, the king and his men live royally without doing any real work. But kings need to watch out. They'll only stay king as long as they're successful raiders. If they are defeated, their men will switch to a leader with more to offer. And not all kings are equal. There are many minor kings like yours, who must each pay tribute to the 'top king' — King Edwin, ruler of the whole of Northumbria.

In a raid, the aim is to seize as much booty as possible from villages in other regions. Gold and silver objects are snatched up, and weapons and armour are stripped from the dead.

Each village has to provide a fixed amount of tribute to the king, and it's the villagers who decide who will pay what. Payments include grain, loaves, cheeses, ale, vats of honey, cattle, poultry and eels.

The king has business to attend to in the village. He judges important lawsuits, collects fines, checks on the work of his local officials and sorts out quarrels between rival thanes.

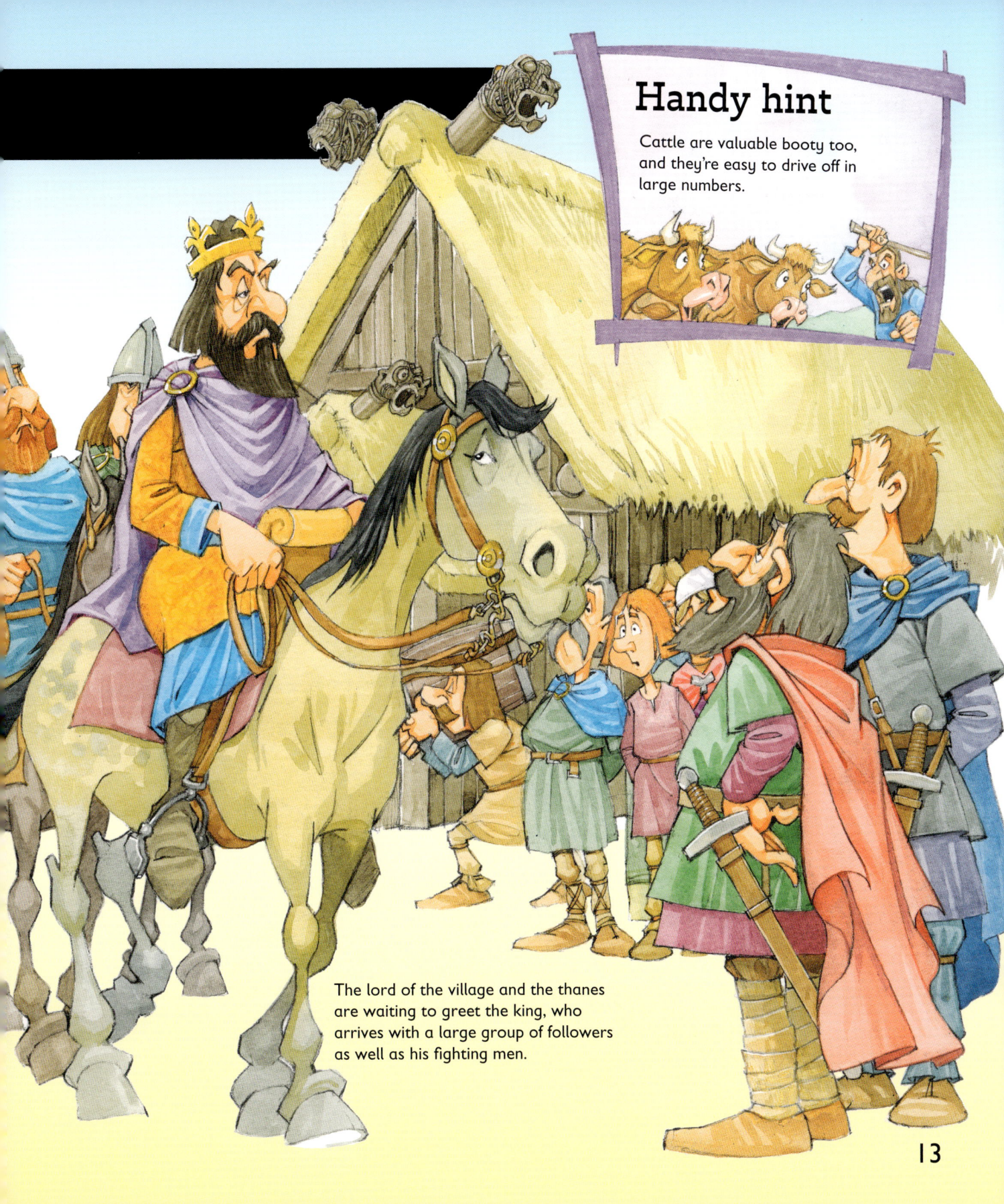

Handy hint

Cattle are valuable booty too, and they're easy to drive off in large numbers.

The lord of the village and the thanes are waiting to greet the king, who arrives with a large group of followers as well as his fighting men.

Going to market

Many of the things you use every day are made at home. Most people in the village can make their own simple coiled pots, which they fire in the village kiln. They make the wooden parts of the tools they need and ask the local blacksmith to fit them with metal cutting edges. Travelling craftsmen sometimes come to the village selling things that need more skill to make, such as metal buckles and finely carved bone combs. But the latest way to buy really high quality things is to visit a market.

These are a new idea. Traders and craftsmen from neighbouring villages set up stalls together at spots where people gather regularly, such as river crossings or important crossroads. The stalls stay up for as long as the fine weather lasts, and people flock to the market to buy and sell. Your father has gone to the market hoping to get a good price for his calves. Your job is to keep an eye on them!

A carpenter is turning a wooden bowl upon a lathe.

A skilled blacksmith is creating a sword blade with a shimmering pattern running down it. The pattern is made from twisted rods of metal placed side by side and hammered together.

There is foreign pottery that looks much neater than the rough pots you make. The seller explains how these are made on a wheel.

You are amazed at the luxuries for sale: Frankish glass beakers and jewellery, bronze bowls and beautiful silks from the Far East. Traders buy these at the coast from foreign merchants.

Handy hint

The smart new way to pay is with coins, not goods. Although your father isn't sure about that...

The old gods

Not long ago, your people worshipped the gods of their ancestors: Woden, king of the gods; Thunor the thunder god; Tiw the war god; and a host of other lesser gods. Christian missionaries have taught the Northumbrians that these are false gods, yet the people in some Anglo-Saxon kingdoms still refuse to give up their old ways. Recently, an East Anglian king was given a pagan burial in great style, in a large boat that had been dragged onto land. A specially prepared chamber within the boat was lined with rich textiles and filled with beautiful and expensive objects worthy of a king. After the funeral ceremony, the royal boat was buried under a huge mound of earth which could be seen from far and wide.

The King is buried with all kinds of impressive treasures, such as a magnificent helmet, a silver spoon and bowl (part of a set of ten) and an elaborately decorated gold belt buckle.

Priests held ceremonies to win the favour of the gods, who were worshipped in temples or in sacred open-air places such as woods or hilltops.

The priests predicted the future based on certain signs. They threw bones on the ground and looked for meanings in the patterns they made.

The coming of Christianity

There is much excitement in the village! The lord has summoned the villagers from all around to make an important announcement. He tells you all that a preacher from Rome, called Paulinus, has come to the court of King Edwin on a special mission. Paulinus has convinced the king that there is only one true god: the god of the Christians. King Edwin has declared that everyone must believe in this god and worship in a new way.

When a powerful king gives orders, you have to obey, but no one knows exactly what they are meant to believe. Christian priests come to the villages to explain that people must be baptised and turn their pagan temples into churches.

A new cross shows everyone that your old temple is now a Christian church.

CHRISTIANITY has been spreading among the Anglo-Saxon kings, ever since Augustine the missionary arrived in 597 and converted the king of Kent. When his daughter came to Northumbria as King Edwin's bride, she brought Paulinus and Christianity with her. Some kings try to combine the new religion with the old. King Raedwald of East Anglia has put a Christian altar in his pagan shrine.

Handy hint

Blocks of stone from Roman ruins come in handy for building a stone church.

The wooden buildings you are used to are not worthy of the great new god. Stonemasons from France and Italy have been called in to teach you how to build in stone.

This is an inscription cut into a sword hilt. It is written in runes, the lettering the pagan priests used and which craftsmen still use to sign their work. It reads 'Sigimer named this sword'.

But it isn't easy to give up old ways. For safety, you still hang a protective charm in the shape of Thunor's hammer around your neck. But you keep it well covered up.

Christian priests can read and write! This is new – no one you know can read or write, not even the king. The priests set up schools in their monasteries to teach the children of noble families.

Priests disapprove of lingering pagan habits such as putting a child in an oven to cure it of a fever – when the oven's cooled down a bit, of course!

Blood feud

Everybody knows everybody else in your village, so they know not just who you are, but also who all your relatives are – your grandparents, uncles, aunts and cousins. These people form your kin, and it is the duty of the whole kin to avenge a wrong done to any of its members. This means that people think twice before committing a crime, because they know their relatives could be in danger once the victim's kin comes seeking revenge.

Anyone caught breaking the law brings shame on every member of their kin. In this way, family honour is used to make sure everybody obeys the law, and this helps to keep life safer in the village. But sometimes things get out of hand, especially between groups of kins from different villages. One act of violence leads to another, creating an unstoppable blood feud. Your family has been caught up in one.

Many years ago, when your grandfather was a young man, a family in the next village accused him of stealing three of their pigs. They would not believe him when he swore that he had not.

This insult to your family's honour had to be avenged, so your grandfather and all his male relatives formed a raiding party and drove away their enemy's pigs and cows.

Handy hint

In a feud, every member of a family is at risk, so always keep your wits about you!

A fire in the night! You wake to find your house ablaze and dash out to escape the choking smoke. But this fire is no accident. It is a tactic to drive your father defenceless from the house. Two men are waiting for him just outside the door, and they attack him before he can escape.

Not surprisingly, that made things worse. The whole of the other kin now felt wronged. Very soon afterwards, your grandfather and uncle were attacked as they were cutting down trees in the forest!

After that, there was no end to the violence! Your father, uncles and all your cousins were caught up in it, as neither family would back down.

The folkmoot

Your family has made a big decision. Instead of continuing the feud with their enemies, they are taking their case to the folkmoot. This is a group of people from villages all around who hold regular open-air meetings to settle local arguments. You demand that your father's killers pay you his 'wergild', which is compensation money that must be paid when someone is unlawfully killed. Everyone has a wergild of a fixed amount. A thane's wergild is eight times more than a ceorl's, a nobleman's is four times more than a thane's, and a king is worth fifteen thanes. Your father's killers are judged to be in the wrong and are told to pay the money. Your family's honour is restored!

Time to pay up!

Each side tells its own version of events. The overlord, acting as the king's representative, is there to make sure the folkmoot keeps to the king's laws.

Sizzle!

Handy hint

Keep in a thane's good books! The folkmoot is more likely to take your side if a thane speaks up for you. His evidence is worth far more than a ceorl's.

If the folkmoot is unable to find out the truth, it will order a 'trial by ordeal'. In an ordeal by fire, the accused person must grasp a red-hot iron bar and carry it for three long strides. After three days their hand is inspected. If it has started to heal, they are thought to be protected by God, which means they are innocent. But if the wound is festering, they are judged to be guilty.

In a trial by water, the accused must pick a stone from a jar of boiling water. If after three days the burn is not healing well, that is a sign of guilt.

The folkmoot usually applies the law with common sense. For instance, there is no punishment for injury in a fight 'when a man finds another man with his wife, daughter, sister or mother behind closed doors or under the same blanket'.

A married woman can ask the folkmoot to support her right to own property and to sell it if she wishes. She cannot be held guilty for any crime committed by her husband. If her husband dies, she is given money to look after her children, as well as a cow in summer and an ox in winter.

A bad year

Growing a year's supply of food is hard at the best of times. It's not too bad in autumn, as there's usually plenty to go around. This is because you can't afford to feed the cattle all through the winter, so many of them are killed beforehand. In spring, there's much less, as stores are low and new crops are not ready – that's in a good year! If the weather is against you, you are helpless. Spring floods make it impossible to sow new crops, and heavy summer rainstorms can ruin the corn, so people have to grind up acorns and bark to make flour. Long drought shrivels up both crops and grass, which means that both people and animals starve.

I can't take much more of this. . .

Nice kitty. . .

When supplies are short, you don't ask what's gone into the stew pot. You swallow it no matter what it tastes like.

When people are desperate and starving they will eat anything – mice, rats, even cats and dogs!

People of high rank are never short of food. Starving ceorl families volunteer to become their lord's slaves, just to get proper meals.

Hunger can be unbearable. It's said that after three years of famine, a group of people from another village joined hands and leapt to their deaths from a cliff top.

The priests tell you that all of these misfortunes are a sign that God is angry with people's wicked ways.

Fighting to the death

The king has asked your lord to bring all the fighting men at his command to help defeat a challenger to the throne. Now that you are twelve, the village treats you as an adult, so you insist on joining the men to fight. Although you're fighting for the king, your first loyalty is to your lord. If he is killed, you must fight to your last gasp to avenge him — it would be seen as shameful to survive the battle without taking vengeance on his killer.

Battles are fought on foot. Each side gathers behind a line of warriors who stand with their shields overlapping to form a defensive wall. The men behind them hurl arrows, spears and throwing axes to make a break in the enemy's shield-wall. Once there is a gap, they rush through and fight the enemy hand-to-hand.

Handy hint

Hold your shield some distance from you. That way, it protects more of your body.

You take an oath of loyalty to your lord by touching the hilt of his sword. You're determined to show such fearlessness that you'll be asked to join his special war band, who live with him in the great hall. You might even eventually achieve the rank of thane.

Every free man owns a spear and most have a knife, a shield and a throwing axe as well. The weight of the axe head and the shortness of its handle allow it to be hurled through the air at great speed. It can strike a man up to 12 metres away.

Only wealthy thanes can afford a sword and chain mail. The richest ones own a helmet, too.

Celebrating victory

A huge feast has been prepared in the great hall to celebrate your side's victory in the battle. The whole village has been invited to join in. The lord, his wife and other nobles are seated at a grand table that runs across the end of the hall. The thanes sit together at long tables running down the middle. Ceorls don't get a seat and instead crowd in along the walls. Slaves scurry about with food and keep the drinking horns topped up. The shouting and laughter dies away as the scop (a story-telling musician) takes up his harp to sing a story of great deeds.

The most important moment in the feast is the gift giving. The lord repays his warriors' loyalty by presenting them with costly armour and weapons seized in battle.

The scop (pronounced as 'shop') sings the story of Hengist and Horsa, your ancestors. The tale may not be exactly true, but it celebrates your history and everyone loves to hear it.

The tale of Hengist and Horsa

Vortigern, leader of the British, asked his council for advice. How could he stop the savage Picts, north of his border, from raiding his lands? The council suggested seeking help from abroad.

Handy hint

If you put a drinking horn down, it will topple over. So empty it in one go!

"It'll cost you..."

Vortigern invited two Saxon warlords, Hengist and Horsa, to bring their men to Britain. They soon put the Picts to flight. But then they wanted payment and refused to leave.

The Saxons saw that Vortigern was weak. More and more of them came over to live in Britain. They terrified the British. Vortigern tried to do a deal with them by marrying Hengist's daughter.

At a feast held to mark peace talks, the Saxons suddenly drew their knives and killed the British nobles! The cowardly Vortigern escaped, but much of Britain now belonged to the victorious Saxons.

Glossary

Angles Settlers from the Angeln region in northern Germany.

Avenge To seek revenge or punish someone for a wrongdoing.

Booty Valuable possessions taken from defeated enemies.

Ceorl A free, low-ranking Anglo-Saxon farmer.

Convert To change a person's religious beliefs.

Embers The glowing remains of a fire.

Festering Oozing pus from a wound.

Feud A long-lasting quarrel between families or kins, usually involving acts of violence and revenge.

Folkmoot A group of local people who discuss local issues and help keep the peace.

Forage To search for food in the wild.

Frankish Coming from the kingdom of the Franks, which was roughly the same as modern France.

Furrow A narrow groove made in the ground by a plough.

Hilt The handle of a sword.

Inscription Words or letters that have been carved into something.

Jutes Settlers from the Jutland peninsular.

Lathe A machine for forming rounded objects from wood.

Legion The basic unit of the Roman army's heavy infantry.

Loom A frame on which cloth is made by weaving threads.

Manure Animal dung that is used to fertilise soil so that crops grow better.

Mead An alcoholic drink made by fermenting honey and water.

Misfortune Bad luck or a distressing and unfortunate event.

Ordeal A painful test to find out if an accused person was guilty or innocent.

Pagan People who continued to worship the old gods instead of converting to Christianity. Anglo-Saxon writers also called them 'heathens'.

Saxons Settlers from the Saxony region in Germany.

Scop An Anglo-Saxon poet-entertainer whose songs celebrated heroic deeds.

Thane A mid-ranking Anglo-Saxon who served an overlord or king.

Tribute An enforced payment of goods to an overlord or sovereign.

Wattle and daub A building material made of interwoven twigs and branches covered with mud, straw and dung.

Wergild The amount of compensation to be paid if someone is unlawfully injured or killed.

Index

A
Angles 5

B
battle tactics 26
bees 11
blacksmithing 14
blood feuds 20, 21
booty 12
bread making 8
Britain, Britons 5, 29
buildings 6, 7, 8, 19

C
carpentry 14
ceorls 6, 13, 24, 28
Christianity 18, 19
coins 15
cooking 8, 9
craftsmen 14

E
East Anglia 5, 16, 19
Edwin, king of Northumbria, 5, 12, 18, 19

F
famine 24, 25
farming 6, 10, 11
fertiliser 11
feuds 20, 21
folkmoot 22, 23

H
Hengist, Saxon warlord 29
houses 6, 8, 9
Horsa, Saxon warlord 29
hunting 11

J
Jutes 5

K
Kent 5, 19
Kins 20

L
lord of village 6, 18, 22, 24, 26, 27, 28

M
markets 14, 15
Mercia 5
missionaries 16, 18

N
Northumbria, Northumbrians 5, 12, 16, 22

O
ordeals 23

P
pagan gods 16
pagan worship 16
Paulinus, missionary 18, 19
Picts 29
ploughs 10
pottery 14
priests 16, 17, 18, 19

R
Raedwald, king of East Anglia 19
raiding 12, 20
Romans 5, 19
runes 19

S
Saxons 5, 29
schools 19
scop 28
ship-burial 16, 17
slaves 6, 9, 28
spinning 9
St Augustin 19
Stonemasons 1

T
thanes 6, 22, 27, 28
thatching 7
tools 14
toothache 9
tribute 12, 13